CANOEING
and SAILING

PHYSICAL EDUCATION ACTIVITIES SERIES

Consulting Editor:
AILEENE LOCKHART
University of Southern California
Los Angeles, California

Evaluation Materials Editor:
JANE A. MOTT
Smith College
Northampton, Massachusetts

ARCHERY, Wayne C. McKinney
BADMINTON, Margaret Varner Bloss
BADMINTON, ADVANCED, Wynn Rogers
BASKETBALL FOR MEN, Glenn Wilkes
BASKETBALL FOR WOMEN, Frances Schaafsma
BIOPHYSICAL VALUES OF MUSCULAR ACTIVITY, E. C. Davis,
    Gene A. Logan, and Wayne C. McKinney
BOWLING, Joan Martin
CANOEING AND SAILING, Linda Vaughn and Richard Stratton
CIRCUIT TRAINING, Robert P. Sorani
CONDITIONING AND BASIC MOVEMENT CONCEPTS, Jane A. Mott
CONTEMPORARY SQUARE DANCE, Patricia A. Phillips
FENCING, Muriel Bower and Torao Mori
FIELD HOCKEY, Anne Delano
FIGURE SKATING, Marion Proctor
FOLK DANCE, Lois Ellfeldt
GOLF, Virginia L. Nance and E. C. Davis
GYMNASTICS FOR MEN, A. Bruce Frederick
GYMNASTICS FOR WOMEN, A. Bruce Frederick
HANDBALL, Michael Yessis
ICE HOCKEY, Don Hayes
JUDO, Daeshik Kim
KARATE AND PERSONAL DEFENSE, Daeshik Kim and Tom Leland
LACROSSE FOR GIRLS AND WOMEN, Anne Delano
MODERN DANCE, Esther E. Pease
RACQUETBALL/PADDLEBALL, Philip E. Allsen and Alan Witbeck
PHYSICAL AND PHYSIOLOGICAL CONDITIONING FOR MEN, Benjamin Ricci
RUGBY, J. Gavin Reid
SKIING, Clayne Jensen and Karl Tucker
SKIN AND SCUBA DIVING, Albert A. Tillman
SOCCER, Richard L. Nelson
SOCCER AND SPEEDBALL FOR WOMEN, Jane A. Mott
SOCIAL DANCE, William F. Pillich
SOFTBALL, Marian E. Kneer and Charles L. McCord
SQUASH RACQUETS, Margaret Varner Bloss and Norman Bramall
SWIMMING, Betty J. Vickers and William J. Vincent
SWIMMING, ADVANCED, James A. Gaughran
TABLE TENNIS, Margaret Varner Bloss and J. R. Harrison
TAP DANCE, Barbara Nash
TENNIS, Joan Johnson and Paul Xanthos
TENNIS, ADVANCED, Chet Murphy
TRACK AND FIELD, Kenneth E. Foreman and Virginia L. Husted
TRAMPOLINING, Jeff T. Hennessy
VOLLEYBALL, Glen H. Egstrom and Frances Schaafsma
WEIGHT TRAINING, Philip J. Rasch
WRESTLING, Arnold Umbach and Warren R. Johnson

PHYSICAL EDUCATION

ACTIVITIES SERIES

CANOEING
and SAILING

LINDA KENT VAUGHAN
Wellesley College
Wellesley, Massachusetts

RICHARD HALE STRATTON

WM. C. BROWN COMPANY PUBLISHERS
DUBUQUE, IOWA

Printed in the United States of America.

Preface

In few sporting activities is the need for the development of basic skills and knowledges more obviously important than in canoeing and sailing. The acquisition of such ability adds both to one's safety and pleasure; to be able to "speak the language" of any sport and to be acquainted with its lore brings enjoyment and deeper respect for the sport. The theory of boating is fascinating. This book has been written to help the reader to understand why a boat behaves as it does and what physical forces and factors he must learn to control in order to produce or harness power and steer in the desired direction. Thus it is hoped that the reader will learn the underlying theory, the purposes and the reasons as well as understand the mechanics of canoeing and sailing.

Self evaluation questions are included in this text. They afford the reader typical examples of the kinds of understanding and levels of skill he should be acquiring as he progresses toward mastery of these activities. The reader should attempt to answer these questions as fully as possible. The reader will find that he can respond more fully and more deeply to these questions, and to others which it is hoped he will pose for himself, as he develops in understanding and proficiency.

The authors express sincere appreciation to those colleagues, faculty and students, who so generously have given advice. Special acknowledgment is given to Miss Diane Mathewson, Wellesley College '69, for her canoeing drawings, and Chrysler Corp. for the use of their sailboats.

Contents

Part 1
Canoeing

Part 2
Sailing

Part I

Canoeing

This section presents a basic approach to canoeing which will serve as a guideline for the development of effective and efficient paddling skills. The author is aware that there is wide variation in the terminology and techniques of canoeing, but all of these can be equally correct for no matter what you call a stroke or how you do it, the desired results are *control* and *safety*.

Information in this section is intended primarily for the beginning canoeist. Some of the material will be of value and interest to the more skilled paddler, while the safety aspects of this sport are applicable to all small craft.

In order to simplify descriptions of skills and to acquaint the reader with the terms used, a glossary has been introduced early. You will probably have to refer to it frequently until you become familiar with the terminology used in the text.

Linda K. Vaughan

What Canoeing Is Like

Anyone who has enjoyed the exhilaration of paddling a canoe on a warm, sunny day in a peaceful, picturesque lake or meandering stream can tell you of the joy of canoeing. The sport itself has a rich heritage going back to the earliest times when man first sought to cross a body of water by fashioning a crude form of dugout boat. Prehistoric man, Indians, Africans and others used various types of canoes whenever there was a need to transport men and supplies for hunting, exploring or traveling. Often a stream or river served as the most efficient means of travel at a time when forests and undergrowth were impenetrable and roads were non-existent.

In modern times canoeing has expanded its role beyond that of transportation into other realms. For example, it is an important part of many summer camp programs where canoes are used for trips, water pageants, and drill teams. Many a summer home has a canoe as part of its basic boating fleet, while hunters and fishermen often use canoes in their quest for game. In addition white water canoeing, racing, and kayaking are further variations of the sport available to those with competitive interests. Though not widely publicized, canoeing even holds a berth in the summer Olympics.

PADDLERS

Before proceeding with the equipment and skills associated with canoeing, there are some important points to make which concern the safety, learning, and skill development of the paddler.

First there is one safety prerequisite for a potential canoeist which cannot be stressed emphatically enough, and that is the ability to swim comfortably in deep water. This applies not only to the paddlers but to passengers as well. The necessity of swimming ability is a matter of good common sense. However, a surprising number of people fail to consider its importance as can be attested by reading about the tragic drownings which are occurring in ever increasing numbers as boating becomes more popular and readily available to the public. In case of capsize, life preservers are helpful in providing additional support, but they were never meant to completely replace swimming ability. This is a basic tool, a skill which may never be used but is absolutely essential in the case of an unexpected incident.

In the process of learning paddling skills you may want to consider the following progression. At the beginning, practice the strokes at the side of the dock or pool by kneeling and paddling in the water. In this way you can concentrate specifically on the strokes and not concern yourself with the canoe, balance, wind, and other problems. Next paddle tandem with a partner so that one person is in the bow and the other in the stern position. Later you can attempt solo, or paddling alone in the canoe.

A third important point to remember is to develop your skills so that you can paddle on *both* sides of the canoe with equal skill and force. This will not only make you a stronger paddler but also a more flexible one who can adapt readily to different paddling situations.

CANOES

Canoes vary widely in size and shape. Most of them range in length from eleven to thirty feet. The standard and most popular length is the sixteen foot canoe which will accommodate three adults. The smaller ones are more suitable for the solo paddler while the larger ones are usually used for guideboats, transporting freight or as war canoes in camps. Some of these larger canoes are able to hold safely quite a heavy load of supplies or a surprising number of people.

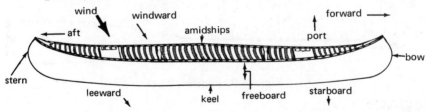

Figure 1A—Canoe Parts and Terminology

Canoes were once constructed of animal skins, hollowed out logs, or birchbark, depending on the natural supply of available materials. Now they may be made of canvas, plywood, rubber, aluminum, fiberglass, or other products. When purchasing a canoe you should consider length, construction, weight, color and other specifics with reference to its proposed use.

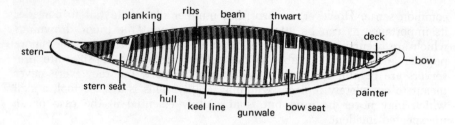

Figure 1B—Canoe Parts and Terminology

PADDLES

Paddles also vary widely in length and shape of the grip and blade. They can be fashioned from softwoods such as spruce, fir, cedar and basswood; or hardwoods such as ash, maple and cherry. Spruce paddles are used most frequently since they are light and easy to handle. The general feel of a blade is a matter of individual preference. Length is potional, but the usual way to measure a paddle is to stand it vertically in front of you and select one which comes to eye level. A slightly longer paddle is better because the added length increases leverage thus making paddling easier and more effective, especially for the stern or solo paddler.

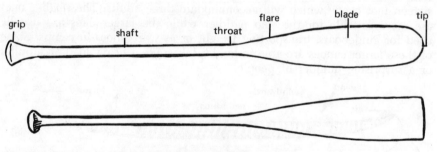

Figure 2—Paddle Parts

SAFETY

Due to the rapidly expanding popularity of boating, more people are purchasing or renting small craft. At the same time statistics referring to accidental drownings associated with careless use of boats, are mounting. Because of this, many state laws now require that United States Coast Guard approved life preservers be readily available for each person in any small craft. Canoeists usually choose life preserver cushions, which serve as cushions for passengers, but can also be thrown to anyone in distress.

For longer trips in unknown waters or for white water canoeing in rapids, U.S.C.G. life jackets are the wiser choice provided they are worn when the water or weather conditions warrant additional safety precautions.

In terms of stability canoeists are advised to assume a position for paddling which is relatively low. For this reason canoes should be purchased without seats. The recommended kneeling position is not as comfortable as sitting on a seat in a canoe, but it is far preferable from a safety standpoint.

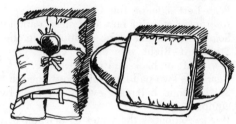

Figure 3—Life Preservers Jacket and Cushion

ACCESSORY EQUIPMENT

There is other equipment associated with canoeing that needs to be mentioned only briefly as it pertains to comfort, to more specific, or advanced aspects of the sport. Since the most stable paddling position is a kneeling one, paddlers may wish to use some type of pad to relieve the pressure on their knees. Rubber mats, sneakers, towels, sweaters, or any makeshift device can serve this purpose. In addition, the following accessories can be readily purchased: poles for traveling in streams where the water is too shallow for paddling, double blades for an introduction to kayaking and speed, a rowing rig to adapt the canoe to a single scull, sailing rig plus associated equipment to convert the canoe to a sailboat and an outboard motor to fit over the side to facilitate travel for the fisherman. As you can see, the versatility of the canoe is endless and fascinating.

Used with proper care and given a program of regular maintenance, a canoe and its accessories can be a lifetime investment. When purchasing equipment follow the manufacturer's instructions. A reputable dealer will gladly assist you if you need additional information regarding maintenance or repair.

LANGUAGE AND LORE OF CANOEING

GENERAL TERMS

Aft—Toward the stern.
Amidships—At the middle or center.
Beam—Point of greatest width of the canoe.

5

Bow—Forward end of canoe.

Broadside—Movement of the canoe as a whole in a sideward direction.

Double blade—Two-bladed paddle of varying lengths and shapes connected at a joint which allows for changing the angles of the blades.

Freeboard—Portion of the hull between the gunwales and waterline.

Forward—Towards the bow.

Leeward—Side or direction away from the wind.

Pivot—Rotary movement of the canoe with each end moving in the opposite direction.

Port—Left side of the Canoe.

Rhythm—Action of bow and stern paddling in unison.

Solo—One paddler alone positioned in the center of the canoe.

Starboard—Right side of the canoe.

Stern—Aft or back end of the canoe.

Tandem—Two paddlers—one positioned in the bow and the other in the stern.

Trim—Canoe balanced evenly on keel by careful positioning of paddlers and equipment.

Wake—Action of the water as a result of canoe movement.

Way—Motion of the canoe forward or backward in the water.

Windward—Side from which the wind is blowing.

CANOE PARTS

Deck—Wood pieces fitted between gunwales at the extreme ends of the canoe.

Gunwale—Top edge extending around the canoe from bow to stern.

Hull—Body of the canoe.

Keel—Outer strip on bottom of canoe in the center extending from bow to stern.

Keel Line—Center line inside the canoe running lengthwise from bow to stern.

Painter—Rope attached to bow and stern.

Planking—Flat sections of wood forming the hull fitted lengthwise next to the canvas.

Ribs—Curved pieces of wood on planking running crosswise.

Thwart—Crosswise supports between gunwales which help canoe maintain its shape.

PADDLE PARTS AND TERMS

Blade—The large flat portion of the paddle.

Grip—Handle of paddle.

Grip Hand—Upper hand located on grip of paddle.

Feather—Flat position of blade in recovery to cut down on wind and water resistance.

Flare—Area of increasing width of paddle where the shaft joins the blade.

Shaft—Long slender portion of the paddle between the blade and the grip.

Shaft Hand—Lower hand located on the shaft of the paddle.

Throat—Junction of shaft with blade above the flare.

Tip—End of paddle at blade.

2

Skills Essential
for Everyone

Anyone can paddle a canoe, but only those who have learned the fundamental skills and knowledge associated with canoeing will ever experience the true sense of satisfaction and enjoyment that comes with the ability to handle a canoe skillfully. The fundamental skills are not difficult to learn and are well worth practicing so you can paddle safely and competently.

CARRYING AND LAUNCHING

Depending on the distance involved from your car or the storage area to the water, the canoe may be carried in a variety of ways; however, the most common practice is to have the paddlers on opposite sides at each end of the canoe supporting it under the bow and stern.

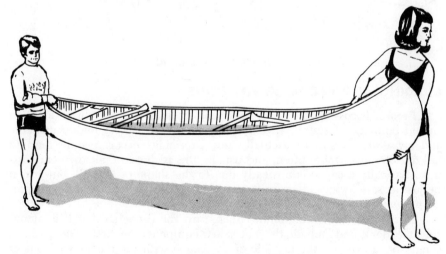

Figure 4—Carrying a Canoe

When ready to launch the canoe in the water you and your partner should position yourselves at either end of the canoe, and carefully flip it over. Gently lower the canoe down on its keel. Then move to the center of the canoe on opposite sides so that you are facing each other. Spread your hands shoulder distance apart, grip the gunwales, bend your knees, and lift the canoe. If launching at a dock, walk to the edge, and place the bow or stern of the canoe in the water so that it slides in at a right angle to the dock. By crossing hand over hand the canoe can be eased gently into the water. Then one person should hold onto the canoe while the other returns for your equipment. If launching at a beach, use the same method or put the canoe only part way in, provided the water is calm, and provided the canoe will be there only briefly. Here the concern is that the hull might become scraped as a result of the rocking action of the canoe in the water.

Figure 5—Launching a Canoe at a Dock

LOADING AND PADDLING POSITIONS

Before discussing the method of getting into a canoe, brief mention should be made of stability. Many people consider canoes highly unstable and consequently unsafe. Actually few capsizings occur; people tend to fall out of canoes more often, and usually this is due to their own carelessness. Basically a canoe is unsteady due to the shape of its hull, but it can be just as safe as any other craft provided you follow this basic principle: *keep your weight centered and low.*

In the case of loading at the dock, turn the canoe so that it is alongside the dock and put all the necessary equipment in first. The paddles should be stowed on the far side of the canoe with the blades well out of

Evaluation Questions

Can you launch a canoe at a beach? at a dock?

the way under the bow and stern decks respectively. After untying the painter, one partner should steady the canoe while the other steps into the middle of the canoe. Take care to step on the keel line and to grasp both gunwales for support. While maintaining a basic crouched position you can move forward or backward in the canoe. After you are situated in a kneeling position in the bow or stern, you can grasp the dock and stabilize the canoe for your partner. It is possible to board a canoe safely from a spot directly opposite a paddling position, but the wisest measure is to enter at the middle where there is the greatest breadth and consequently the most stability. If there should be a passenger, he should be assisted into position in the middle of the canoe first. Because of this, the paddlers may wish then to board directly at the bow or the stern.

When loading a canoe from a beach, slide it into the water bow first, trying to get as much of it into the water as possible. As the bow paddler,

Figure 6—Loading a Canoe at a Dock

you should step directly over the keel in the canoe being careful to avoid putting any weight on an area of the hull that is still resting on land or under which there is an air pocket. Stay over the keel line, grasp the gunwales on both sides, and move forward slowly. Your sternman can stabilize his end of the canoe by straddling the deck and reaching forward to grasp each gunwale while bracing the canoe between his knees. Passengers may enter next, and should exercise the same care while moving into position. Before entering the canoe, you can push it out away from shore to avoid grounding it. After wading out, put one foot in, grasp both gunwales, and push off with the rear foot. If the canoe still remains on land, the stern paddler should move forward temporarily until the stern drifts free.

Figure 7—Loading a Canoe at a Beach

UNLOADING

After stowing the paddles, assume a crouching position with your feet straddling the keel line and one hand on each gunwale. Step onto the dock with the nearest foot moving your hands from the far gunwale to the near one. Then shift your weight onto that foot, and move the other foot onto the dock. Be sure to maintain contact with the canoe with your hands to prevent loss of balance. Take the painter and secure the canoe to the dock using an appropriate knot for the type of fastening found there. Then remove the equipment from the canoe. Avoid the habit of carelessly throwing paddles and equipment onto the dock. This creates hazards for other people and can result in damage to the equipment. If there are passengers, the paddlers should stabilize the canoe by holding onto the dock and let them out first. If a passenger is an older person, one paddler should get out first and assist the passenger from the canoe.

In the case of landing and unloading on the shore, bring the canoe in gently, bow first, and step out when the bow of the canoe softly strikes bottom. As bowman, you can then draw the canoe up a little further and rest your end of the canoe on the beach so that it is partially out of the water. Equipment and supplies can be passed forward by the sternman and unloaded. Then passengers and the sternman can move forward carefully in the center, utilizing the gunwales for support and step out over either side of the bow. With one person on either side, the canoe can be drawn out of the water and carried to the proper storage area.

Another method of landing and unloading, if you don't mind wet feet, is to turn the canoe so that it is parallel to the beach rather than bringing it in bow first, and unload it from this position.

If the canoe is not going to be used again, it should be removed from the water and stored properly. Untie the canoe and swing one end of it away so that it is perpendicular to the dock. Reach down and grasp the canoe with one hand under the keel, the other hand under the deck, and lift it out of the water. One person should be on either side standing at the edge of the dock. Crossing hand over hand, lift the canoe out of the water until you and your partner are opposite one another at the middle of the canoe. It is important to be careful not to let the canoe seesaw, whereby the end bounces off the dock. Staying at the midsection on opposite sides of the canoe, walk to the storage area and lower the canoe gently to the ground. Move to either end, lift the canoe, flip it over and replace it on the racks.

If the canoe is to be carried some distance, it can either be transported with a paddler at each end as described earlier, or carried upside down on the shoulders. Refer to any books on canoe camping for more detailed descriptions of the manner in which this portage technique is employed.

PADDLING SKILLS

Once you are in position and ready to begin paddling, each of you should move closer to your paddling side in order to facilitate the strokes and distribute the weight evenly. Since paddling is always done on opposite sides, this will serve to "trim ship" as well as preserve the gunwales from chaffing.

The correct manner in which to hold a paddle is to place the lower hand nearest your paddling side around the shaft above the flare. It is preferable to keep your hand high enough so that it remains out of the water on each stroke, but low enough to permit full range of motion. Your grip or top hand comfortably wraps over the top of the grip so that your fingers are away from you.

In a resting position, the paddles can be stowed under the decks or held across the gunwales. Since most people have a preferred side or find themselves getting tired due to continuous paddling on the same side, the paddles can be lifted up and over the canoe, grips shifted, and the strokes can be resumed on the opposite side. When there are extremely cold conditions, or passengers, you should attempt to shake most of the water off the blade before changing sides.

STRAIGHTAWAY—The straightaway is the basic stroke used to give the canoe forward impetus. Extend the paddle blade straight ahead without changing your basic grip or body position. Your grip hand should start at shoulder level with the elbow bent down, lower arm straight. As the blade enters the water, pull straight back with the lower (shaft) hand, and push the top (grip) hand away with equal force. As you do this action, think in terms of leverage with an imaginary fulcrum located midway up the shaft of the paddle. By exerting an equal push-pull action, you should feel the power exerted by the blade as it moves through the water. At the completion of the stroke the blade is lifted from the water in a feathered position. Your fingernails will be facing down toward the water. Keeping the blade flat and low, swing it forward and keep the elbow of the lower arm relatively straight on the recovery. Then flip the blade so that it is in position to begin a new stroke. There is a rhythm to paddling which you will begin to establish for yourself. Usually the bowman sets pace and the stern paddler follows suit so that you are paddling together "in rhythm."

BACKWATER—The backwater stroke is used to move the canoe backwards toward the direction of the stern. To execute this stroke extend the paddle straight back with your fingers facing down, insert the blade in the water, and then push it forward. By equalizing the pushing force of

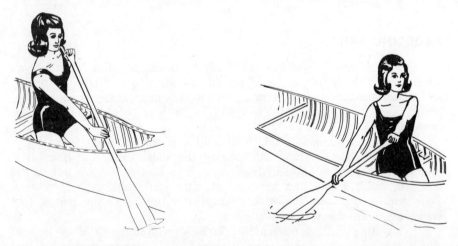

Figure 8—Straightaway—Beginning   *Figure 8—Straightaway—Completion*

the shaft hand and the pulling action of the grip hand, leverage can be applied. The trick is to try to keep the shaft of the paddle as perpendicular to the water as possible. This will necessitate getting your grip hand out over the water when doing the stroke. At the completion of the stroke the blade will be facing up. To put it in a feathered position for the recovery, turn the fingers of the grip hand down and then swing the paddle back to its original position.

HOLD—The hold stroke is used to prevent any further headway. One way to stop a canoe is to stroke in direct opposition to the stroke you were doing. For example, if the canoe is moving forward, do a backwater which is the opposite of a straightaway. Another way to accomplish this is to hold the paddle horizontally across the canoe. Then, push the grip hand straight up and across your body while pulling the shaft against the canoe with your lower hand. Make sure that the flat part of the blade is facing forward. The heel of the shaft hand may be rested on the gunwale for additional stability, but under no circumstances should you hook your thumb on the gunwale. Given enough force this might be the cause of a painful sprain or dislocation. To stop sideward motion do a slight action in opposition to the previous one; i.e., a draw if the original stroke was a pushaway. In this case, be sure the flat part of the blade is parallel to the side of the canoe so that the blade is in a position of greatest resistance to the direction of movement.

DRAW—This draw or pull-to is used to change the direction of the canoe. Depending upon the combination of strokes selected by the bow and stern paddler, the canoe can be made to pivot or broadside as a result of this stroke.

To move your end of the canoe in the direction of your paddling side, maintain the position of your hands on the paddle and lower the grip hand with your fingers up and extend the blade out in line with your hip with the flat portion of the blade facing the canoe. Insert the blade into the water and then as you push the grip hand across your body towards the water, pull the lower portion of the paddle toward the canoe with the shaft hand so that there is an equal push-pull action. Imagine the gunwale acting as a fulcrum. The paddle blade can be removed from the water on the recovery, but it is preferable and faster to keep it in the water and use an underwater recovery. At the completion of the drawing action, the blade is next to or slightly under the canoe. Turn the fingers of the grip hand in order to rotate the blade one quarter of a turn in either direction. The blade is now in position with its edge against the canoe. Raise the shaft hand and lower the grip hand simultaneously to slice the blade back through the water. Twist the grip back, and the paddle is in position to draw again. The blade should remain in the water throughout the stroke and recovery. When utilizing a lot of force, care must be taken not to let the blade get trapped under the hull at the completion of the stroke. If the paddle does get swept under the canoe, the natural reaction of most paddlers is to hold on tightly with both hands and subsequently lose their balance. If this should occur, as it often does in the early learning stages, merely release your hold on the grip, but maintain contact with the shaft hand. Don't be afraid to let the paddle go slightly beyond a vertical position at the completion of the stroke, but keep a fairly firm grip for control.

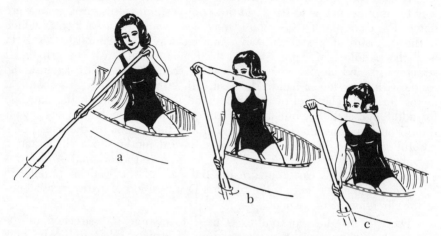

Figure 9—Draw Stroke—Beginning, Completion, Recovery

PUSHAWAY—This stroke is used to push the canoe away from your paddling side; in other words, it has the opposite effect of the draw stroke. To execute the stroke, insert the blade straight down and slightly under the canoe so that the flat part faces the side of the canoe. The grip hand should be out over the water as if you were trying to pry the canoe loose with the paddle. Then push with the shaft hand and pull down with the grip hand employing equal pressure with both hands. As in the draw, imagine the use of the gunwale as a fulcrum. At the completion of this action while the blade is still in the water, turn your grip hand so that the blade moves one quarter of a turn in either direction. The edge of the blade will be facing the hull, then slice it back through the water for the recovery. When the blade has returned to a position slightly under the canoe again, turn it back to a flat position and repeat the stroke. A helpful hint is to get the paddle in a position slightly beyond the perpendicular so that the blade is closer to the keel; this will result in a more powerful stroke.

J-STROKE—This is a steering stroke used by the stern man in maintaining a straight course to offset the sideward motion of the canoe resulting from the wind or the stern paddler's own strokes. It should be

Evaluation Questions

Do you know how to get in and out of a canoe safely when you are alone? when you have a passenger?

executed in such a way as to complement the momentum of the canoe and adjust to the direction of the canoe without disturbing the rhythm of the paddlers or impeding the forward progress of the craft. The stroke turns the bow of the canoe toward the stern's paddling side. Paddling on port, begin the stroke as if you were doing a straightaway, and as the paddle reaches the vicinity of your hips, start turning the blade away from the canoe by turning the grip in a clockwise direction. In so doing, your wrists will begin to round or flex. In the process of turning the blade, exert continual pressure against the water in an outward-backward motion by pushing with the shaft hand and pulling toward you with the grip hand. At the completion of the stroke, the blade will be in a position with the flat part of the blade parallel to the side of the canoe. Lift the blade out of the water, flatten or relax your wrists to feather the blade so that it is facing the water surface and recover it forward so that a new stroke may be started. In order for the J-stroke to be effective it is important to get the grip hand out over the water to allow the blade to remain as close to the keel as possible and allow the paddler to reach as far back as possible. Because the canoe tapers at the ends, care will have to be taken to keep the blade in close. A series of quick J-strokes should accomplish the desired steering action while allowing the stern to keep in rhythm with the bow. A prolonged J, which is actually a rudder, will cause the canoe to veer sharply, conflicting with the forward momentum and making paddling more difficult for the bow. Lack of flexibility in the wrists may inhibit the range of motion as to the angle of the blade, but with practice any tightness or discomfort will gradually disappear. Paddlers differ as to the manner in which the J-stroke is done. While the prime feature of the stroke is control, the least tiring and most effective interpretation will become a matter of individual style.

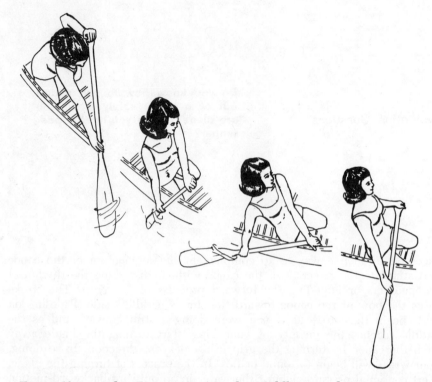

Figure 10—g-stroke—Beginning of Stroke, Middle, Completion, Recovery

SWEEP STROKES—Another stroke of importance to the stern paddler for steering purposes is the forward sweep which will turn the bow away from the stern's paddling side without severely affecting the canoe's established pace. With the grip hand at waist level and the flat portion of the blade facing forward, extend the paddle to the side in line with your hip and perform a horizontal sweeping motion back toward the stern. Pull with the bottom hand and push horizontally out with the grip hand to employ leverage. This stroke done in rhythm with the bow may be used along with the J-stroke and the straightaway to maintain a straight course.

The opposite action from that described above for the stern paddler is a reverse sweep. Be sure to reach well back, and keep the paddle on a horizontal plane while sweeping forward from the stern to a position opposite your hip. This will cause the bow to move toward the side on which the stroke is done.

For the bow paddler the sweep will be the same except for minor adaptations due to the positions of the two paddlers in relation to the ends of the canoe. In the forward sweep, the range of motion will be from the bow back to your hip and not beyond. Any movement toward

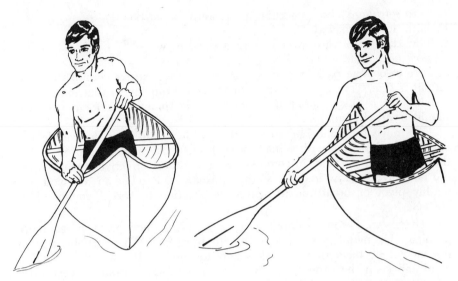

Figure 11—Sweep Stroke in the
Bow—Beginning

Figure 11—Sweep Stroke in the
Bow—Completion

the middle of the canoe by either paddler tends to result in an overlap of effort with relatively little effect.

The reverse sweep can be done in the bow but it is relatively ineffective and awkward due to the required range of movement and body position which obstructs leverage. The only force which can be applied is a pushing action with the lower arm. The body interferes with the action of the grip hand.

STRAIGHT COURSE—A good way to determine the effectiveness of your steering strokes is to set your sights on a specific object such as a tree or building and see if you can establish and maintain a straight course toward this object. Do the same thing while trying to move backwards. In the case of tandem paddling, the sternman usually set the course and advises the bow of adjustments to be made such as paddling harder or doing a slight draw in order to maintain the desired direction. Both paddlers should be in rhythm in order to establish a basic momentum which will facilitate this maneuver.

PIVOT TURNS AND BROADSIDING—In order to pivot the canoe to port or starboard, these basic strokes may be combined as follows:

Turn to port (bow paddling port, stern on starboard)

1. both paddlers do a draw
2. bow does a reverse sweep, stern a forward sweep
3. bow does a backwater, stern a straightaway

17

Turn to starboard (bow paddling port, stern on starboard)
1. both do a pushaway
2. bow does a forward sweep, stern a reverse sweep
3. bow does a straightaway, stern a backwater

Be sure to change paddling sides and try the same stroke combinations on the other side. Try to pivot to port or starboard quickly so that it becomes a matter of reaction rather than considerable thought. Tandem paddlers should be in rhythm.

To move the canoe broadside, the paddlers will need to paddle not only in rhythm, but with equal force. From a stationary position, using the draw and pushaway in combination is the most effective; for example, the bow does a draw and the stern a pushaway. Practice so that you can readily pivot or broadside the canoe in reaction to verbal command or obstacles.

DIAGONAL LANDING—Landing a canoe at a dock often poses more problems for paddlers than returning to the shore. This may be due to the mental obstacle that a dock seems to convey. If you allow for the wind and keep the canoe under control, you should encounter very little difficulty.

On an approach to the dock, position the canoe so that you are coming in on an angle and if possible try to keep the bow heading into the wind. This will assist in slowing the momentum. Come in slowly and aim the bow at a specific point. The stern should advise the bow of the desired strokes, which will assist the landing procedure. Upon nearing the dock, gently steer the bow away and glide in so that the canoe slides in parallel and next to the dock. Keep your paddles in the water and execute the necessary holdwater maneuver to prevent any further motion. Many a canoeist has approached a dock with too much speed and lost control of the canoe, resulting in a crash landing, a damaged canoe, and two very embarrassed paddlers. Also, in their eagerness to land, people reach out and grasp the dock to slow themselves down rather than using the paddles to complete the landing maneuver. The result can be a painful splinter or a finger caught in the dock.

SUMMARY—Given the proper understanding of these skills, the would-be canoeist can now launch and load a canoe properly. You can paddle forward, backward, and turn the canoe by utilizing the draws, pushaways, and sweeps in combination. By altering the selection of the strokes just mentioned, the canoe can be maneuvered broadside as well. And you should now be able to paddle straight forward to a predetermined location, and land safely either at a dock or beach.

3

Better Canoeists Master These Techiques

Upon becoming more proficient and confident you may wish to add these techniques to your canoeing repertoire. For example, the rudders are stationary strokes in which the paddle is put in the water at a specific angle and position and held. Depending upon the speed of the canoe and the strokes executed by the stern, the canoe will either sideslip or pivot while continuing its forward progress. The rudders are usually associated with river paddling in which the bowman is responsible for watching for obstructions and submerged hazards and is expected to advise the stern as to the location of these so that the proper action may be taken to prevent collision.

BOW RUDDER

The bow paddler does a bow rudder in the following way. Remain in a kneeling position braced against the thwart or seat. Extend the paddle forward on the same side on which you are paddling and insert the blade in the water close to the bow with the top edge slightly angled away from it so that the flat portion of the blade faces the canoe. The shaft hand can remain low so that the shaft is either in contact with the gunwale or not while the grip hand is braced against the shoulder with the elbow tight against the body or up in line with the shaft acting as an extension of it. Preferably the shaft hand slides slightly up so that the heel of the hand is braced against the gunwale. The position of the paddle should be well stabilized while the angle of the blade acts as a trap and causes the bow to veer to that direction. Note that if the blade is inserted too far away from the bow, it is apt to get caught in the momentum and it will be imposible to hold the paddle in the desired position.

CROSS BOW RUDDER—This is done on the opposite paddling side without changing your original grip on the paddle. Swing the blade over the bow of the canoe and slice it into the water on the other side in approximately the same position as the bow rudder with the same edge on top. Your grip hand will be at waist level away from the body. While doing the stroke, twist your upper trunk and face that side of the canoe. The lower hand and shaft need not be in contact with the gunwale unless you find it easier to brace yourself.

STERN STROKES FOR THE BOW RUDDERS—As a stern paddler, you can select from a variety of strokes that will cause the canoe to move away from or toward your paddling side resulting in a pivoting or broadsiding action. In some cases it may be desirable to pivot the canoe as in a head-on landing, sudden obstruction, or formation paddling. However, in the case of an obstruction, pivoting the canoe may swing the bow away only to endanger the stern with imminent collision. Therefore you must be familiar with all the strokes and fully aware of their effect when done in combination with the bow paddler's action so that you can pivot or broadside the canoe quickly when necessary.

For example, in conjunction with the bow rudder, you can elect to do a series of rapid draws with an over or under water recovery or a series of forward sweeps to cause the canoe to pivot. For a broadsiding action, a series of pushaways, reverse sweeps, or just holding the paddle over the stern as in a rudder could be utilized. Paddlers soon developed a preference for the strokes they like best, but the important factor for success is speed. The action of the wind, water and strokes utilized are all contributing factors to speed. Once the forward momentum of the canoe is

Figure 12—Bow Rudder

Figure 13—Cross Bow Rudder

interrupted and the speed begins to taper off, the effectiveness of your strokes will also wane. The initial action has the greatest sustaining effect on the course of the canoe; therefore it must be done correctly. Try these at a moderate speed when first learning them, but upon becoming more confident, speed up and notice how much more powerful your actions become.

SCULLING

There are many forms of sculling such as the C or W, but the most commonly used is the figure 8. Forward sculling causes the canoe to move toward your paddling side, whereas reverse sculling has the opposite effect. Place the paddle in the water so that the blade is facing the side of the canoe. The usual point of reference is in line with your hip. Be sure that the blade is fairly vertical in the water. The grip hand controls the angle of the blade while the lower hand moves the paddle back and forth in the water. Now do a slight draw toward the canoe, then cut the blade diagonally forward and away from the canoe so that it is once again in the starting position for a draw but a little more toward the direction of the bow. Draw again and recover the blade by sliding it diagonally out and back toward the stern until it is in its original position to draw again. This pattern only encompasses an area of about one foot. As you are doing the action just described, turn the grip hand so that the edges of the stroke are rounded off and a small figure 8 pattern becomes apparent in the water. Resistance or pressure should be felt continually throughout the stroke so that it feels as if you are pulling the water toward the canoe with the paddle. Reverse sculling is basically the same except that the starting action is a push-away rather than a draw and it is done closer to the side of the canoe. The smooth rhythm of sculling is sometimes a little more difficult to establish but a little extra practice will help you achieve this in no time.

CHANGING PADDLING POSITIONS

If you are not near a dock and it is absolutely necessary to change positions it is advisable to try to do this in shallow water. By moving slowly and cautiously, an exchange can be done quite easily and safely, but it is recommended for more experienced paddlers. First, the paddles should be stowed so that they will not be a hazard. Then, the bow paddler moves back to the center of the canoe by assuming a crouching position and holding onto the gunwales for support. At a balanced position in the center, huddle down in the bottom of the canoe as compactly as possible. A passenger, if any, should do the same. The sternman then moves forward straddling you and the passenger and works toward the bow holding onto

21

When changing places in a canoe, which of these foot positions (in relation to the keel) is safer?

Evaluation Questions
CHANGING PLACES

the gunwales *at all times*. After the bow position is assumed, you may continue backing to the stern, straddling the passenger, if any, in the process. After the new positions are established, paddles can be exchanged. The main factors are to keep your weight centered and low and to use the gunwales for support. Move in the center of the canoe whenever possible except when passing over the paddler or passengers.

DOCK LANDINGS

Basically the idea on landings is to develop the ability to come in from any direction, under any conditions, either solo or tandem, and bring the canoe to a stationary position beside the dock without bumping it or feeling the need to reach out to fend it off or grab hold of it. It takes patience and practice but the canoeists who can consistently land smoothly and confidently will gain a great deal of personal satisfaction.

Dock landings can be generally classified into three categories: slide or diagonal, parallel or broadside, and head-on. A slide landing, which was previously described in Chapter II, is a manner of coming into the dock from an angle and sliding into a position of dead stop. Try this at various speeds and under a variety of weather conditions. Remember that the key factor is control.

A parallel or broadside landing is done by coming toward the dock to within a distance of about three to six feet, stopping, and then broadsiding the canoe to a position beside the dock.

Head-on landings are usually done in such a way that the canoe approaches the dock perpendicularly and pivots at the last instant so that it ends up alongside the dock. This can be done at a slow speed by utilizing the conventional draws, pushaways, and sweeps; or it can be

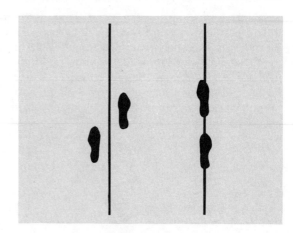

Diagram A

CHANGING PLACES

done at high speeds with a bow or cross bow rudder provided the stern executes a stroke which will create a pivot action. If done incorrectly, the latter method can turn into a crash landing which may seriously damage the canoe, so it is recommended only for expert paddlers.

SOLO PADDLING

As you become more skillful and confident in tandem paddling, solo experience will further develop your skills. This is due to the fact that you become solely responsible for the action of the canoe. If your strokes are ineffective, you will find it difficult to control the craft. However, there are some adaptations which will facilitate learning solo paddling. These are described briefly in this section.

POSITION—Depending on the length of the canoe and the consequent position of the thwarts, take a balanced kneeling position in the center of the canoe and lean against the thwart using it as a brace. Be careful not to sit on a thwart; it was not meant to support your weight and could easily break under the strain. Since you are the only paddler, you can disregard the bow and stern and face either direction. Your knees can be together or they can be apart if a slightly wider base of support is desired. Some paddlers like to straddle a rolled towel, a sleeping bag, or any other soft padding. A half kneeling position often referred to as the relief position is preferred by many. In this case, you should be kneeling on the knee nearest your paddling side with the other leg bent or extended so that the foot is flat and either toeing in across the keel or toeing out while braced against a rib. Try to get close to your paddling side; this will put the canoe slightly off balance, so that the gunwale on that side will be lower. This will facilitate paddling due to less interference from the gunwale and the fact that the action of the blade can be accomplished in a closer relationship to the keel. As you become more experienced, you may wish to have the canoe off balance more so that the gunwale on your paddling side is almost down to the water. This is recommended only if you are comfortable and completely in control of your balance. Any sudden movement while in this position might cause the canoe to swamp or capsize.

Figure 14A–Solo Paddling
–Relief Position

Figure 14B–Solo Paddling–
Kneeling Position

MODIFIED STRAIGHTAWAY—Since only one side of the canoe is utilized in paddling, a longer paddle is preferable for control while adaptations in the strokes and the basic force employed will have to be made to offset the action of a single paddle. The modified straightaway is basically an adaptation of several tandem strokes for use by the solo paddler to move the canoe forward. Reach ahead and away from the canoe as if starting a conventional straightaway. However, add a slight diagonal drawing action to the beginning of the stroke so that the path of the paddle is one of moving diagonally toward the canoe; then continue in a straightaway alongside and end in a J-stroke. Recovery is the same as for the regular straightaway. Essentially then the stroke is merely a straightaway into which a slight draw at the beginning and J-stroke at the end have been incorporated.

In solo paddling, smooth rhythmical strokes and a balanced canoe will help establish a basic momentum which will in turn produce the best effect from the strokes and facilitate control of the craft.

SWEEPS—The sweep stroke adapted for the solo paddler may now encompass an entire side of the canoe of a 180° range as opposed to the

Evaluation Questions

While paddling solo, can you steer a straight course, pivot, broadside, and land the canoe?

previous 90° range in tandem paddling. It is helpful to slide the lower hand up the shaft of the paddle in order to increase the range of motion by utilizing a longer lever. Place the paddle in horizontal position in the water. Reach forward and sweep out and back as far as possible to get maximal effect. This stroke can be done as a forward or reverse sweep to turn the canoe away from or toward your paddling side, respectively. But it is easier merely to change paddling sides and utilize only the forward sweep as it is more effective than the reverse. This is due to interference in the range of motion by the body position. The forward sweep stroke can be developed further by swinging the blade across the canoe and doing a slight sweep toward the canoe on the other side, then jumping the paddle back over the canoe and continuing in a full forward sweep stroke. This can be done either before or after the full sweep. The grip remains the same throughout the entire stroke even when the paddle is temporarily on the wrong side of the canoe. This stroke is sometimes called the outside pivot turn and serves to give an added impetus to the action of the sweep.

OTHER STROKES—When paddling solo, any of the tandem strokes may be utilized individually or in combination. It must be realized that the action of the strokes in relationship to the center or ends of the canoe will influence the type of effect these strokes will have. For example, a draw done in line with the center of the canoe will result in a broadsiding action, whereas the same stroke done closer to the bow or stern will have a pivotal effect. Draws, pushaways, sweeps, rudders, and other strokes can all be utilized in solo paddling. Note that bow and cross bow rudders done from the solo position amidships will result more in a sideslipping, broadside action. The hold stroke is not particularly effective for stopping a solo canoe, but can be used to slow the canoe down.

PADDLING IN WIND AND ROUGH WEATHER

Depending upon its force and severity, wind may present difficulties to inexperienced paddlers. A wise canoeist will learn to regard the natural elements with a deep respect. Mention is made here of techniques to be used to aid paddlers in wind conditions, but the wisest measure is not to venture out at all in questionable weather.

TANDEM—In case of strong wind and rough water, tandem paddlers will find it wise to seek a position of greater stability in the center of the canoe. This will also tend to lighten the ends of the canoe so that they ride higher and ship less water. You can then kneel or sit and continue paddling or head for shore. Paddling on the leeward side is helpful, especially for the sternman; and if the wind is strong enough, both paddlers may have to be on the same side, although this is not too advisable. If your paddling efforts are to little or no avail, then the only resort is to wait out the storm by sitting or lying down in the canoe. But if the waves are sizeable, it is wise to try at least to keep one end of the canoe into the wind rather than letting it swing broadside. This can be done by dragging a paddle over the bow or stern as a rudder.

SOLO—If the wind is not too strong, remain in the center and paddle on the leeward side on a diagonal path into or with the wind. Otherwise move forward or backward in the canoe and weight down the end of the canoe from which the wind is blowing. For example, when paddling into the wind move forward, but avoid going too far into the area of the bow or stern where the canoe becomes extremely narrow and consequently unstable. Then try to establish which paddling side is the most satisfactory in terms of stroke effectiveness and stay with it. A great deal depends on the paddler's skill, strength, position, and the severity of the weather conditions. To move in the direction of the wind, move back in the canoe. By weighting down the end of the canoe into the wind, the canoe will become more stable and the lighter end will act as a weather vane and swing in the path of the wind. If it is a steady force, this will assist the paddler in steering. When the conditions are more violent, such as in the case of a severe storm and you are unable to make any headway, stay in the center of the canoe and lie down in the bottom to ride out the storm.

CAPSIZE PROCEDURE

If you fall out of a canoe, be sure to maintain contact with it if possible. Re-entry should be made at the middle of the canoe due to its greater breadth and greater stability. Hold onto the closest gunwale and kick your legs up to a horizontal position in the water. Then press down on the near gunwale and reach for the far one or the far side of a thwart. Keeping the elbow up, kick yourself across and into the canoe, then roll and let your hips drop inside. Resume paddling, or, if the paddle has been lost, kneel down and hand paddled, using your hand and forearm. If there are two people, one can stabilize the canoe for the other as he attempts to get back in.

It is difficult to swamp or capsize a canoe intentionally, but when it happens accidentally, there are several procedures which can be followed. One is to leave the craft in a swamped upside down position and hang onto it for support. If the canoe is not far from shore, swim to safety by pushing it. Otherwise you can roll the canoe right side up and then gently reach inside and press your hands down in the center. Assume a horizontal position in the water and carefully swim into the canoe. Moving slowly, sit on the bottom and hand paddle. A canoe full of water is highly unstable so that any movements should be slow and controlled, but the craft will support all the previous occupants despite its swamped condition. No matter what, always remember the basic safety rule: *stay with your craft.* It is a life preserver and will support you indefinitely. Never abandon a canoe and try to swim to shore. You may find you have placed your life in jeopardy because of the sudden realization that you are not as strong a swimmer as you thought, or the distance to shore was greater than you anticipated.

4

Progress Can Be
Speeded Up

The following maneuvers can be done either solo or tandem and are helpful in reinforcing the basic skills. In addition, they will help you gain more confidence and experience:

ENDURANCE

Try to paddle for prolonged periods of time or a prescribed distance, maintain a continuous pace, and change sides only at a specific time or point. This is to develop endurance and equal skill on both sides in paddling. These factors are especially important if you are contemplating a trip or any other paddle of appreciable distance. You are the only source of power for your craft and consequently need to be in good physical condition.

MAZE PADDLING

Using such equipment as plastic gallon size bleach bottles, styrofoam floats, lily pads, and moored boats; a maze course can be devised for paddling practice. The pattern can be in a straight line or more complicated so that certain strokes are required. The object is to maneuver the canoe skillfully through the maze in an attempt to avoid the buoys. A time factor can be added so that it becomes not only a matter of skill but speed.

FORMATION PADDLING

A single canoe can outline a specific pattern in the water such as a figure eight. This is best done on a calm day when the wake of the canoe can be seen easily. Another type of formation paddling can be a game of follow the leader, with each canoe following the first one's path.

Some of the patterns which might be used are as follows:

Circle—form a large circle, bow to stern, with all canoes moving forward or backward to give the effect of a wheel.

Star—start from the circle formation, turn the bows to center, then move the canoes carefully forward until the bows touch, then back out.

Shuttle—form two parallel lines facing one another. Canoes move across and pass between each other. Continue on through and then do the same in reverse.

Figure 8—outline a figure 8 pattern of varying sizes in the water.

RACING

Control of a canoe can be further enhanced by adding the competitive element of time. A race can be set up as a straight or slalom course for one, two, four, or more paddlers per canoe. Further novelty variations are also possible such as paddling backwards, hand paddling, using brooms, or jumping out and re-entering on a whistle signal. Anyone with imagination can elaborate on these novelty events, but safety should always be considered when planning them.

DOUBLE BLADE

If you have an opportunity to try a double blade, it is fun and it gives you a little insight into what kayaking might be like. This can be done either solo or tandem. Primarily both sides of the canoe are used, and the strokes are more of a forward or reverse sweep action. You will notice that the action of the blades will give you more speed once you get under way. The blades are used in a horizontal sweeping action alternately on each side, the more vertical your stroke action becomes the more water runs down the shaft to dampen you and the inside of the canoe. The blades can be set so that they are at right angles to one another. This will position the blades so that as one is in the water, the other will be in a feathered position for recovery. The wrists control the angle of the blade as it enters the water.

Rules of Canoeing

1. Know your craft and your ability and stay within these limits.
2. Paddlers and passengers should be able to *swim in deep water.*
3. There should be an appropriate life preserver for *each* person in the canoe.
4. Never overload a canoe.

29

5. Avoid shifting your weight suddenly or leaning out.
6. *Never* go out on the water during a thunder or electrical storm.
7. Check weather conditions before leaving. Be aware of unusual cloud formations, sudden shift in the wind, a falling barometer, or revised weather forecasts.
8. Be sure you have left word of your destination and estimated time of return.
9. Stay close to shore whenever possible.
10. Avoid cumbersome or heavy clothing. Wearing apparel should be capable of being easily removed.
11. *Do not* canoe after dark unless you have adequate and appropriate lights which will warn other craft of your presence.
12. In case of a sudden storm, head for shore immediately.
13. If caught in a severe storm, stay low and try to keep one end of the canoe pointed into the waves. Otherwise move to the center and lie down.
14. If you capsize stay with the canoe. It will act as a natural life preserver. *Do not* attempt to swim to shore.
15. On a trip, be sure to carry extra paddles, a first aid kit, repair kit, and flashlight.
16. Above all use common sense!

Unwritten Laws and Etiquette

1. Be sure to do your share of the paddling. The sternman who drags his paddle as a rudder to steer rather than utilizing a J-stroke and lets the bowman do all the work will quickly find himself without a partner in the future.
2. Wear appropriate clothing and have something light which is wind and waterproof in case of inclement weather. Sweatshirts are a poor choice for trips because they are difficult to dry out once they get wet.
3. Trips require *endurance*. Good canoeists try to be sure they are in sound physical condition by paddling to develop stamina before attempting a trip of any appreciable distance.
4. White water canoeing calls for special skills and know-how. If you wish to avoid the risk of swamping a canoe full of equipment or damaging your craft, seek expert advice.
5. Damaged equipment cannot serve you well. Learn the proper care and maintenance of your paddle and canoe.
6. Treat all rental or borrowed equipment as if it were your own so that others may enjoy its use as much as you.
7. Abide by posted regulations wherever you see them—especially if you are renting a canoe.

8. Horesplay may lead to a dunking, injury, or serious harm to an un-suspecting party. Set a good example.
9. Inexperienced paddlers should never take a canoe out alone unless they plan to practice under supervision.
10. Courtesy, common sense, and know-how will leave a more favorable impression in the long run.

Now You Are Canoeing

With your new abilities you can now paddle on your favorite lake, stream, or ocean bay. A reputable company or rental agency can be readily ascertained upon inquiry if you wish to purchase or merely rent equipment.

For many, the lure of exploring for its own sake, fishing, hunting, or camping are avenues of adventure which can be pursued by means of a canoe. On an extended trip in remote areas be sure you have an ex-perienced guide or clear your intentions with the local ranger. There is much to learn regarding proper equipment for camping, food supplies, and planning your trip route.

White water canoeing is a sport which attracts those who love the thrill of turbulent waters and the element of risk. The skills of this sport can be learned through programs sponsored by such organizations as the Appalachian Mountain Club, the Sierra Club, Outing Clubs, and other local groups. The important factor is to learn the basic skills before challenging white water conditons.

Kayaking is another version of canoeing. Here again specific skills need to be learned. Usually there is a club or organization which sponsors this in the form of pleasure or competitive events. The amount of activity available in either of these latter areas is contingent upon locale. For those of you who might be interested, a list of national organizations has been included in the selected references at the end of this chapter. These are established groups from which additional information regarding local white water or kayak clubs might be obtained.

Basically canoeing is a sport or activty for all ages. It can offer a pleasant, restful excursion or the challenge of strength and skill necessary to maneuver rapids. The canoe itself has a wonderful potential in terms of varied use. Enjoy it and share your pleasure with others.

SELECTED REFERENCES

BOOKS

American National Red Cross. *Canoeing.* New York: Doubleday and Company, 1956.

ELVEDT, RUTH. *Canoeing A–Z.* Minneapolis: Burgess Publishing Company, 1964.

New England Camping Association. *Canoeing Standards and Graded Classifications.* Somersworth: Somersworth Free Press, 1958.

PULLING, PIERRE. *Principles of Canoeing.* New York: MacMillan Company, 1954.

RUSSELL, CHARLES W. (ed.). *Basic Canoeing.* American Red Cross, 1963.

URBAN, JOHN T. *A White Water Handbook for Canoe and Kayak.* Boston: Appalachian Mountain Club, 1965.

ORGANIZATIONS

American Camping Association. Bradford Woods, Martinsville, Indiana 46151.

American Canoeing Association. 1217 Spring Garden Street, Philadelphia, Pennsylvania 12123.

American National Red Cross. Local Chapter.

Appalachian Mountain Club. 5 Joy Street, Boston, Massachusetts 02100. The American White Water Affiliation.

Sierra Club. 1050 Mills Tower, San Francisco, California 94104.

Part II

Sailing

Becoming an expert sailor is rather difficult. It comes only with hours of practice, under many varied conditons. But learning how to sail is relatively easy once the mystery is solved by removing the nautical jargon and installing the common understandable words.

A student can learn the basics in a few short hours, understand the concept almost immediately, and be sailing by the time he completes this booklet.

All that is needed is water, wind, and a sailboat.

Richard H. Stratton

5

The Sailboat-
Terms and Types

Most people learn how to sail in a small simple sailboat; one with a hull, a mast, a rudder, a centerboard, a mainsail and a jib. By using these few nautical terms some of you may already be lost. Look at Illustration 1 which shows the nomenclature of a small sailboat. Use this illustration as a reference when an item is mentioned which you don't understand.

Only by the combined efforts of the skipper and his crew can a boat be sailed correctly. All commands the skipper gives must be fully understood and obeyed by the crew. These terms may seem strange and even somewhat ridiculous to the beginner. But for common understanding they must be used. A nautical glossary may be found at the end of this booklet.

The average small sailboat has a fiberglass hull with two sails (main and jib), which is called "sloop rigged." The forward part of the boat is called the *bow*; the back end is the *stern*. So you can see, to go toward the bow is going forward but going toward the stern is going *aft*. While facing the bow of the boat, the right-hand side is called the *starboard*; the left-hand side is called the *port*. On the starboard side of the boat green is used as an identifying color, while red is used on the port. A centerboard on a small boat prevents the boat from drifting laterally while under sail. The other parts can be identified in Illustration 1.

There are many types of sailboats afloat today. All of these cannot be covered in this booklet, but we will explain the four (4) basic types of monohull sailboats.

1. The Sloop   3. The Ketch
2. The Yawl   4. The Schooner

These boats are classified and identified by the position of their masts. As you can see in Illustration 2, the single-masted boat is called a *sloop*. There are many types of rigs which a sloop may carry.

Two-masted vessels are called *yawls*, *ketches*, or *schooners*. The placement of the masts and their respective, comparative heights are the factors

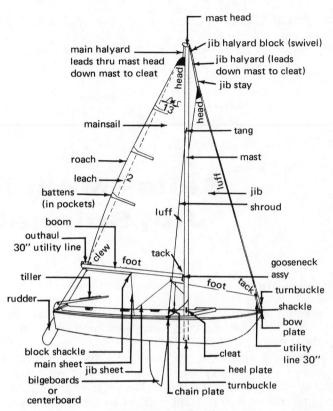

Illustration No. 1.

which determine which type each is. The yawl has its smaller mast, the mizzen or jigger, behind the mainmast and aft of the tiller or steering apparatus. The ketch has its mizzen or jigger behind the mainmast but forward of the tiller or steering apparatus. The schooner has its smaller mast, or foremast, forward of the mainmast. Each of these types of boats also have many types of rigs under which they sail.

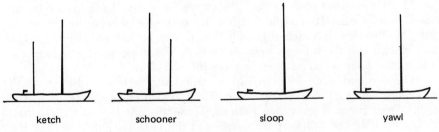

Illustration No. 2—Types of Sailboats

6

Sails—Main and Jib, Spinnaker

MAINSAIL AND JIB

The working sails on a sailboat are called the mainsail and the jib. These sails are called the working sails because they do the work of making the boat go.

Most all working sails today are made of a polyester synthetic cloth, commonly known as Dacron. They resist mildew and rot, which plagued the old canvas sails we used to have. Dacron sails are also difficult to stain or soil and are very strong and hard to stretch out of shape.

As you can see by Illustration 3, the smaller sail is the jib and the larger is the main. The jib is always forward of the main.

Each sail has a head, tack, and clew. The mainsail is connected to the boom at the foot and secured at the clew by an outhaul. It is secured to the boom and mast at the tack by a gooseneck. The main halyard is connected to the head and is used to hoist the sail in place. Tensions can be adjusted on the mainsail by adjusting the outhaul at the clew, the downhaul at the tack, and the halyard at the head.

The jib is connected to the jibstay, or headstay, by clips or snaps, called pistol hanks. Its tack is secured, by way of a shackle, to the stemplate. To the clew is attached the jib sheets. The jib halyard is attached to the jib head and the sail can then be hoisted. This process of attaching the sails to the boat is called "bending on the sails."

The forward edge of each sail is called the luff, and this you will hear more about in chapters to come. The wooden or plastic sticks at the leach of the mainsail are called battens. These are installed in their batten pockets to help the sail keep its shape and not curl around to deflect the air. Picture 1 shows a boat sailing with its working sails.

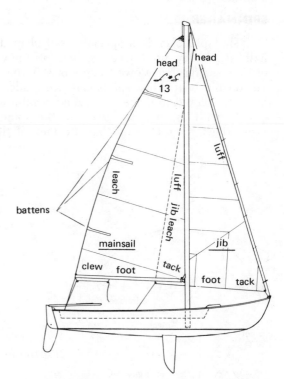

Illustration No. 3.

Picture No. 1.

SPINNAKER

The spinnaker is a specialty sail shaped like a large balloon cut in half. It is only used when sailing off-the-wind. It improves the speed of sailboats on their slowest angle of sail, the run. It is normally the largest sail on the boat. Most spinnakers are made of lightweight nylon and are brightly colored to make a weekend regatta a camera bug's delight.

As with the mainsail and jib, the spinnaker has its head, tack and clew. Illustration 4 shows that the tack of the spinnaker is attached to a

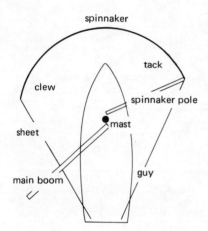

Illustration No. 4—Spinnaker Rig

spinnaker pole, which in turn is connected to the mast. The "guy" line is always on the pole side. The spinnaker sheet is attached to the clew. And, as on the working sails, the head is attached to the halyard for hoisting. Since it is so large and bulky, it is smart to hoist it out of a bag or box. The big sail is controlled by combined trimming of the sheet and guy.

To raise the chute, as the spinnaker is commonly known, you attach the halyard, the sheet and the guy to it while it is still in its bag or box. You then attach the spinnaker pole to the mast and guy, stationing it at the desired height by use of your toping lift. Hoist your sail to a point near the top of the mast and give a tug on your sheet and guy. As the wind catches in the big chute, it will fill. (See Illustration 5.)

Lower it in behind the mainsail when you change your angle of sail to an on-the-wind course. Picture 2 shows a boat sailing with a spinnaker.

SAILS—MAIN AND JIB, SPINNAKER

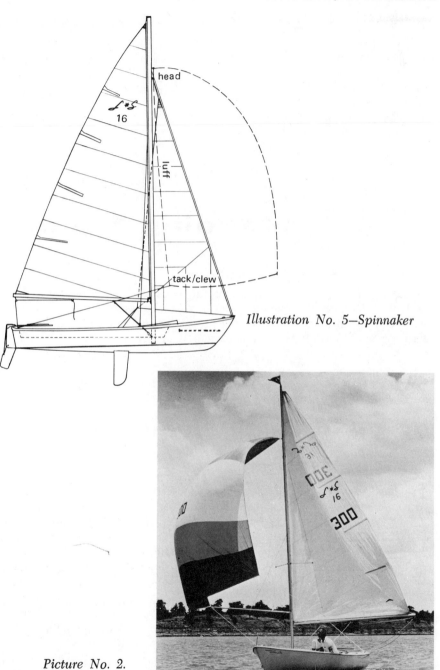

Illustration No. 5—Spinnaker

Picture No. 2.

7

Standing Rigging

The standing rigging consists of the headstay, the backstay and the shrouds. It "stands" permanently as long as the mast is up, holding the mast securely in place. This rigging is usually composed of stainless steel wire, wrapped in strands, so it is extremely strong. (See Illustration 6.)

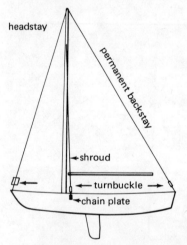

Illustration No. 6—Standing Rigging

Some boats have permanent backstays, some movable backstays, and some no backstays at all.

If the headstay runs from the bow to the top of the mast, this is called a mast headed rig.

The stays that run from each side of the boat to the mast are called shrouds.

Evaluation Questions

To judge the effect of aerodynamic force, what factors must you consider and why? What other forces must you also consider in sailing?

All stays attach to the boat's hull by means of stay adjusters or turn-buckles. These may be adjusted to get the tension which is desired. The stay adjusters or turnbuckles secure the shrouds to metal chainplates built into the hull.

When the mast is too long to be held direct by stays, a set of spreaders are added to the standing rigging. Spreaders are small metal struts extending from both sides of the mast aloft. The shrouds lead over the ends of these struts and then to the mast at an angle, providing a stronger rig.

The higher a mast on larger sailboats, the more types of standing rigging are needed.

Running Rigging

Running rigging refers to the lines used to raise and control the sails. By lines we mean rope. When rope is used on a sailboat, it is termed a line. The running rigging consists of halyards, sheets and guys, all movable and "running" about the boat. The halyards are the lines used to hoist the sails up and down. The sheets are the lines which move the sails in and out. Each sail has its own halyard and sheets. (See Illustration 7.)

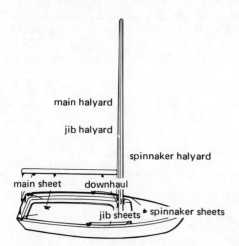

Illustration No. 7—Running Rigging

The halyard after being shackled to the head of the sail goes up the mast and around a pulley and back down to where it is cleated. Halyards must be kept clear and readily available so they can be lowered fast in any emergency.

The main sheet is a single piece of line running into the cockpit through a group of pulleys or blocks, while the jib sheets are a double piece of line, one coming in from each side of the mast.

Running rigging is the control center of the boat, so they should be inspected often and kept in perfect operating condition at all times.

When you are feeding the sheets through the pulleys and blocks they belong in, this is called reeving.

Other items which make up the running rigging family are: guys, topping lifts, outhauls and downhauls. The guy helps control the spinnaker as mentioned previously. There are two types of topping lifts: one which raises the main boom (on larger boats only) and one which raises the spinnaker pole. The main boom topping lift is usually used, when the mainsail is not up, only to support the boom. The lift on the spinnaker runs from the center of the spinnaker pole to a pulley on the mast, to a cleat on the mast. A spinnaker downhaul runs from the center of the spinnaker pole to a cleat on the deck. This prevents the sail from flying too high. The main downhaul is connected by the gooseneck on the inboard end of the boom. This pulls down the tack of the mainsail, therefore assuring the tension desired in the luff of the sail. The main outhaul is connected to the clew of the mainsail to achieve the desired tension on the foot of the sail.

9

Angles of Sail

In order to steer a boat on a desired course, no matter what direction the wind is coming from, requires discussion of the angle of sail. A sailboat is capable of sailing into the wind (BEATING), sailing at right angles to the wind (REACHING), and sailing with the wind (RUNNING). These three points of sail, along with the reaching variations, can be done on either tack. (See Illustration 8.) In all of these angles of sail the wind will first contact the sail at the luff and thrust off the sail at the leach. (See Illustration 10.)

Beating is sailing as close to the direction of the wind as possible. This is about 45° off the wind.

Reaching is sailing at right angles to the wind. This is 90° off the wind.

Running is sailing downwind or with the wind pushing you. This is 180° off the wind.

(See Illustration 9 for these points of sail.)

To explain briefly how you trim the sails for the angle in which you want the boat to go, a simple rule is: Let out the sheets until the luff of the sail begins to flutter. Then pull the sheets in until the fluttering stops. If you have held course during this time, you have then trimmed the sails for the direction in which you are going. Since the wind is always changing, it is a good practice to do this exercise quite often to be sure you have the right trim.

BEATING

For the novice, the most difficult angle of sail to understand is beating. How in the world can a sailboat sail into the wind? Well, it was done for quite a few years before anyone could understand why. It was

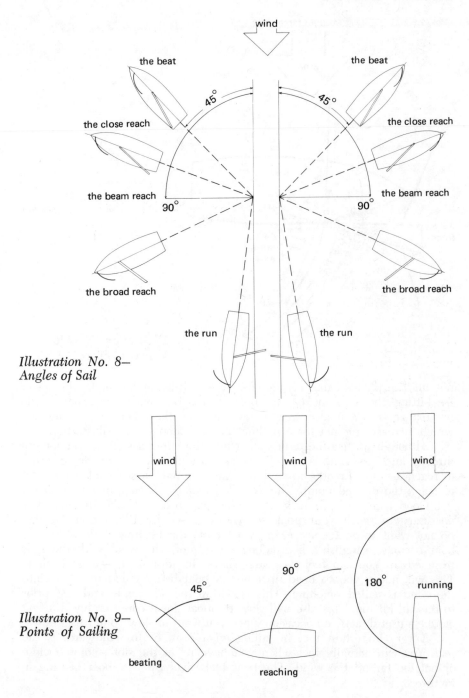

Illustration No. 8—
Angles of Sail

Illustration No. 9—
Points of Sailing

45

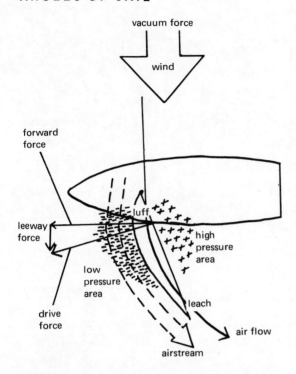

Illustration No. 10—
Vacuum Force

not until airplanes came of age that it was fully understood. The wind, by hitting the sail, makes the boat move. But what most people do not realize is that it also creates a vacuum on the other side of the sail, which increases the net force pulling the boat along. (See Illustration 10.)

Although we use the term sailing into the wind, a sailboat cannot sail directly into the wind. About 45° is as close as you can go. So, in order to reach a point directly upwind you have to make a series of maneuvers to reach the desired point. This is called *tacking*. (See Illustration 15.)

Good trim on each tack is essential in order to make the headway necessary to reach your goal. As you can see by Illustration 11, you do not want to go too close, or two far off the beating angle of sail. A boat becomes sluggish when sailing too far off the wind with the sails trimmed in. You can feel this sluggishness in addition to excess heeling. This will notify you to head up more. A boat being sailed too close into the wind is called pinching. This is within the 45° angle and just prior to the sail luffing. This also will slow the boat down considerably. Luffing can be a useful tactic on occasion when you want to slow your vessel down.

A very important fact in sailing on a beat, or to windward, is the *feel*. You can actually feel when you have it "in the slot"—not too close or not too far off the wind. The boat feels lively. See a boat beating in Picture 3.

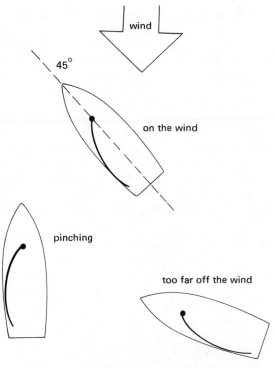

wind

45°

on the wind

pinching

too far off the wind

Illustration No. 11—
Beating

1547

Picture No. 3.

To guarantee that you are "in the slot" when beating, first be sure your sails are trimmed correctly. Then, while holding this trim, head the boat up into the wind until you read a luff on the jib or main. Once you see this luff begin, immediately head off so the sails are full again. Do this again and again, each time checking your direction and you can see, if you have a compass, that the wind does vary and your direction will vary slightly on almost every occasion.

When beating, you will realize your greatest angle of heel. (See Picture 4.) Due to the wind force on the sail, the boat will tend to lean over. The first counter force for this is the centerboard, which protrudes into the water giving the boat stability. If the wind is too strong for the centerboard alone to counteract this heeling, you may have to make your crew hike out. (See Picture 5.) By this we mean balance their weight to offset the heeling or leaning over. Things to remember when beating:

1. Your centerboard should be all the way down.
2. Your sails are trimmed in towards the center of the boat, or tight.
3. You are sailing as close to the wind as possible, without pinching.
4. You do not fall too far off the wind.
5. You distribute crew weight to counteract heel.

Picture No. 4.

Picture No. 5.

REACHING

A sailing course between beating and running is called *reaching*. This is the easiest and fastest angle of sail. A beam reach is 90° off the wind. Picture 6. Any angle between 90° and 45° off the wind is called a close reach. Picture 7. Any angle of sail between 90° and 180° is called a broad reach. Picture 8. (See Illustration 12 showing the reaches.)

Picture No. 6.

Picture No. 8.

Picture No. 7.

Can you adjust your sails properly for reaching? for running? for beating?

Evaluation Questions

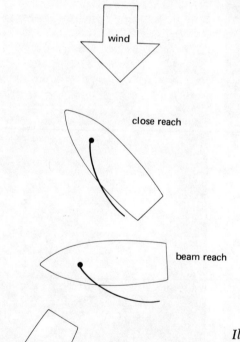

wind

close reach

beam reach

broad reach

Illustration No. 12—Reaching

You have to "start" or let out the sails when going from beating to reaching. The farther you are off the wind, the more you let the sails out.

Reaching is fairly trouble free as long as the wind is not overpowering. Long reaches can sometimes get quite monotonous, so most people like to use spinnakers on reaches. This can be done as long as it is not too close a reach. This angle of sail is probably the best for novices to start out on.

The correct sail adjustment for the angle of reaching is the same as in beating: Let them out until they luff; pull them in until they stop luffing. Always keeping the same course or heading. Remember if the sails are trimmed either too tight or too loose, the boat will lose speed.

RUNNING

Moving in the same direction as the wind is called running. Other terms used for this angle of sail are called: downwind, downhill, off the wind, before the wind, and free. You should expose as much of the sails' surface to the wind as possible. In other words, let the mainsail out as far as it will go. (See Illustration 13.) When running, the boat should

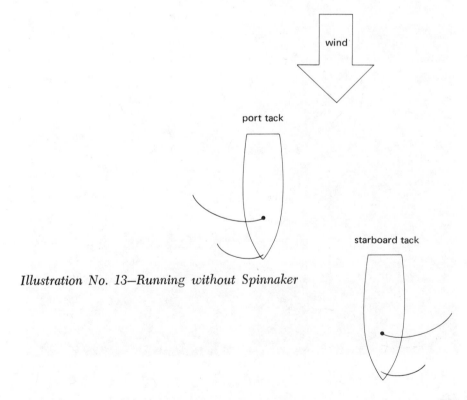

Illustration No. 13—Running without Spinnaker

travel as fast as the wind pushing it, less the resistance of water drag. This is not quite true, but very nearly when the spinnaker sail is used.

The spinnaker, being the large balloon-type sail bellowing out in front of the boat, turns this slow lazy angle of sailing into a really nice ride. See Picture 9. Some boats do not carry spinnakers though; so they fly their jib on the opposite side of the boat than their main, exposing as much sail surface to the wind as possible. This is called sailing "wing and wing." See Picture 10. When sailing wing and wing, a pole is used from the mast to the clew of the jib to hold it out in place. This is called a wisker pole.

Except when there is excessive wind, running is an easy angle of sail. When the wind is up, the helmsman must steer a straight downwind course. If the wind should change or if a sea roll should swing the stern around, a dangerous uncontrollable jibe could take place. A jibe is when the wind gets behind the mainsail and forces it to the other side of the boat.

A novice sailor should practice sailing on a broad reach before he starts running in a good breeze.

Picture No. 9.

Picture No. 10.

TACKING

To come about or tack is to change direction of the sailboat and head off on a new course. Tacking requires changing the sails from one side of boat to the other side. If you are sailing on a port tack and then change to sail on a starboard tack, by swinging the bow through the wind you are tacking. See Illustration 14. When you swing the bow through

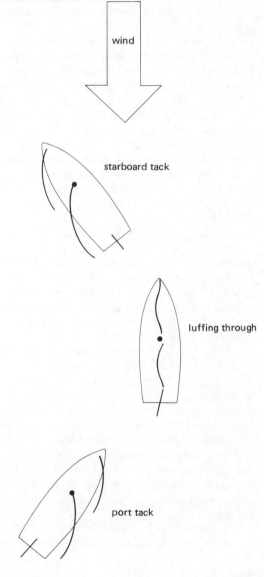

wind

starboard tack

luffing through

port tack

Illustration No. 14—Tacking or Coming About

the wind in the middle of a tack, you lose all pulling power. So, be sure you have enough speed to coast through this luffing period and complete your tack. If you do get caught halfway between tacks and you cannot go to either tack, you are said to be "in irons."

The best way to get out of irons is to grab the jib by the clew, and hold it out against the wind, on the opposite side of the boat in which you want the boat to head.

When you want to come about or tack, you have to notify all hands. This is done by a preparatory command which is "Ready about." The command indicating action which follows shortly is "Hard-a-lee." This tells the crew that the tiller is being moved hard to the lee of the boat, therefore making the bow swing into and through the wind. While this is happening, the crew frees the jib sheet, and the wind then carries it across the midship of the boat as the crew pulls the jib sheet in on the other side. The mainsail also goes from one side of the center of the boat to the other. But if you are not going to head off the wind more on your new tack, you do not have to change the mainsail setting. The tack is over when the boat reaches its new course and the jib is sheeted down. Do not stand up in the boat when changing tacks, or the boom will get you. If you have to change positions while tacking, do so without standing. Illustration 15 shows a boat tacking to windward.

JIBING

Turning the bow of the boat away from the wind, rather than into it, when changing tacks is called jibing. This is usually done when sailing downwind or running. As the wind catches on the back side of the sail, the boom and mainsail will swing across the cockpit of the boat. This crossover happens much faster in jibing than in tacking, and the sail swings a greater distance. (See Illustration 16.)

Unlike a boat losing speed when it comes about, a boat jibing usually gains speed.

The preparatory command given by the skipper to the crew is "Prepare to jibe." Then he swings the tiller to windward and gives the command for action "Jibe ho." The bow falls off the wind and the mainsail is hauled in as fast as possible to control the crossover. When the wind catches it on the new side, then let the sheet out so the sail will be trimmed on the new tack. This is a controlled jibe. A flying jibe is when you allow the wind to move the sail from one side of the boat to the other, without first pulling the sheet in and then letting it out again. Only competent yachtsmen should use flying jibes. The jibe is completed when the skipper has the vessel on its new course and the tiller is again amidships. Jibes can go wrong, so they should always be deliberate and controlled.

Jibing with the spinnaker up is a little more difficult and should not be attempted by beginners. It takes hours of practice to complete this

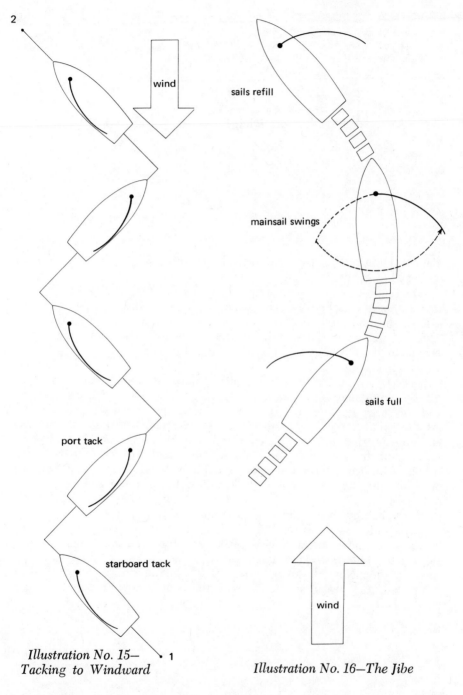

2

wind

sails refill

mainsail swings

port tack

sails full

starboard tack

Illustration No. 15—
Tacking to Windward

1

Illustration No. 16—The Jibe

wind

What are the first three steps in preparing the boat for sailing?

Evaluation Questions

maneuver correctly. By studying Illustration 17, you can follow the sequence of events in jibing the spinnaker.

In Figure 1 you see the spinnaker flying on starboard tack. You know it is starboard tack because the spinnaker pole is on the starboard (RIGHT) side of the boat and the main boom is on the port (LEFT) side of the boat. As the wind shifts and goes more toward your port quarter, you decide to hold course and jibe the spinnaker.

As the skipper moves the tiller to windward, the bow of the boat swings away from the wind. This should be done slowly. (See Figure 2.) At the same time, one crew member holds both the sheet and the guy, and the other goes to the foredeck to move the spinnaker pole. He lets off the spinnaker pole downhaul, takes the spinnaker pole off the mast and attaches that end to the clew of the sail. While the boat is still slowly turning, he removes the pole from the tack and secures it to the mast. At this same time, the crew member holding the sheet and guy is paying or letting the sheet slowly out while pulling the guy slowly in. The mainsail jibes the same as normal, swinging from one side to the other, while the cockpit crew hands duck. (See Figure 3.)

The old clew becomes the new tack and vice versa. The old sheet becomes the new guy and vice versa. The foredeck crew member then secures the pole downhaul and returns to the cockpit to man either the sheet or guy. Now the skipper puts his helm amidship and the jibe is completed. As you can see in Figure 4, the boat is now on port tack.

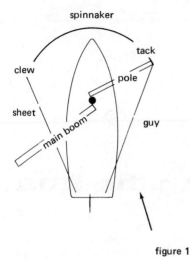

figure 1

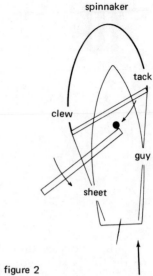

figure 2

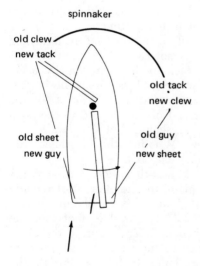

figure 3

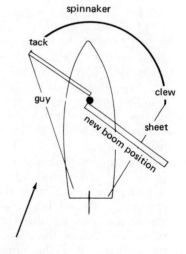

figure 4

Illustration No. 17—Jibing the Spinnaker

10

Rigging the Boat

Most novices find it confusing when first learning how to prepare or rig the boat to go sailing. After doing it a few times, it becomes old hat. Doing it in the right sequential order to start with will make it that much easier to learn.

The very first thing you do when preparing the boat to go sailing is to lower the centerboard, that is, if it is a centerboard boat. This stabilizes the boat so you can move around it freely. Attach the rudder and tiller next. Then check to see that all your sheets and halyards are not tangled. Do not remove the boom crotch at this time.

Let's bend on the jib first. Bending a sail on the boat means attaching it. Take the jib by the tack and be sure it is not twisted by running your hand up the luff to the head. Secure the tack to the stemplate by using a shackle. Snap or clip the luff of the jib on the jibstay from the bottom up. Free the halyard from the mast and be sure it is clear of all the standing rigging. Attach the shackle at the end of the halyard to the head of the jib. Do not hoist at this time. After seeing that the foot is not twisted, attach the jib sheets to the clew. Whether the jib sheets run inside or outside of the shrouds differs on each boat.

The mainsail should now be checked to see that there are no twists in the foot or luff. Taking the foot of the main, by the clew, start feeding it along the boom from the inboard end. Since this small boat had a grooved mast and boom, you insert the sail rope on the foot into the groove and pull towards the end of the boom. Before securing the clew, secure the tack at the gooseneck. Now back to the clew and secure it to the outhaul. Pull the outhaul until it is hand taut. Now install the battens in the pockets at the leach of the sail. If there are no twists in the luff, attach the head to the shackle at the end of the main halyard. Naturally, it is necessary to see that the halyard is clear of all standing rigging.

58

Hoist the main first, to the top of the mast, without binding it in the masthead. Adjust any slack in the sail by pulling down on the downhaul, then secure it. With the main sheet free, the sail will not power the boat. Remove the boom crotch and stow it. Now hoist the jib, making sure before doing so that the jib halyard is clear. Halyards should always be double checked. They seem to have a way of fouling themselves at the most inopportune time. Once the jib is "sweated up" or pulled real tight so there are no scallops in the luff of the sail, secure the jib halyard. Securing the main and jib halyards and stowing the excess line in an orderly fashion is very important. You never know when you have to let the sails down fast. A knotted up halyard can cause all types of problems. You are now ready to cast off and trim the sheets for sailing!

11

Rules of the Road

In almost all instances, sailboats have the right of way over power-boats. But it is sometimes necessary to abandon these rules and just use plain common sense. The primary purpose of the rules of the road is to avoid collision between two craft. Although these rules were written to control water traffic, unfortunately there are many people on the water today who do not know the rules.

The rules cover all meetings, crossings, and convergings; and they establish which vessel must keep clear of the other.

It is written, "The power driven vessel shall keep out of the way of the sailing vessel." But, please don't pick on the Queen Mary in your 14 foot sailboat. There are two exceptions to this rule, though. First, all vessels, including sailboats, must keep clear of any boat fishing with nets, lines or trawls. And, second, when a sailboat overtakes a moving powerboat, the sailboat must keep clear. Common sense will tell you not to force your sailing right of way in other instances, like a large power-boat maneuvering in tight quarters or a tug boat pulling a line of barges, etc.

The general sailboat rule as two sailboats converge is: "A vessel which has the wind aft shall keep out of the way of the other vessel." Additional basic rules are shown in Illustrations 18, 19, 20, 21, and 22. Also see Picture 11.

Remember, it is better to give up your right of way than be dead right.

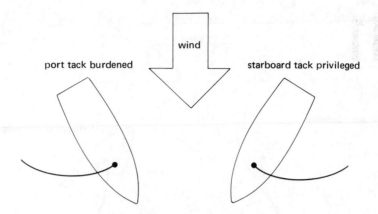

When both are running free, with the wind on different sides, the vessel which has the wind on the port side shall keep out of the way of the other boat.

Illustration No. 18—Rules of the Road

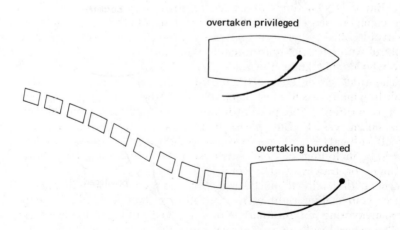

Every vessel overtaking any other shall keep out of the way of the overtaken vessel.

Illustration No. 19—Rules of the Road

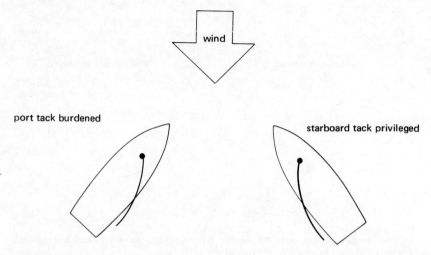

port tack burdened

starboard tack privileged

A vessel which is close-hauled on the port tack shall keep out of the way of a vessel which is close-hauled on the starboard tack.

Illustration No. 20—Rules of the Road

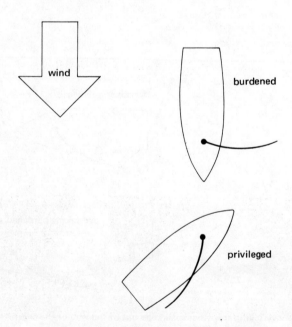

wind

burdened

privileged

A vessel which is running free shall keep out of the way of a vessel which is close-hauled.

Illustration No. 21—Rules of the Road

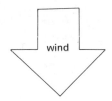

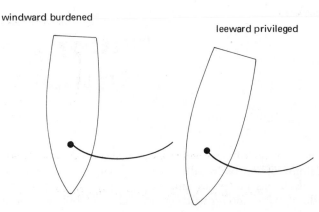

When both are running free with the wind on the same side, the vessel which is to the windward shall keep out of the way of the vessel which is to leeward.

Illustration No. 22—Rules of the Road

Picture No. 11—Every Vessel Overtaking any Other Shall Keep Out of the Way of the Overtaken Vessel

63

12

Fittings and Equipment

FITTINGS

All the items of hardware aboard a sailboat are called fittings. They come in varied shapes and sizes and are priced according to the material they are made of. Most modern fittings are made of bronze, chrome, aluminum, or stainless steel.

The most common hardware used on a small boat is listed below.

Stemplate—What your headstay turnbuckle or stay adjuster is attached to.

Turnbuckle—An adjustable fitting which connects your stays to the plates on a sailboat.

Bow Chock—What you lead your mooring line through to tie up your boat.

Cleats—A horn-eared fitting to which you secure a line. Cleats used on sheets which can be removed fast have a cam action and they are called cam cleats.

Shackle—What you use to attach your halyards to the heads of your sail with. Also used on the tack and clew of the jib. A horseshoe-shaped fitting with a through bolt closing the open side.

Gooseneck—This secures the boom to the mast.

Boom Vang—A pulley arrangement which runs from the bottom of the boom 1/3 of the way out, to a spot near the bottom of the mast. It keeps the boom from rising when running.

Fairleads—Eyelets which deflect the direction of a line.

Block—Acts instead of a fairlead with a pulley inside the eyelet.

Winch—A mechanical device used to haul in sheets or haul up halyards.

Pintles—Male fittings attached to the rudder for securing to the transom of a boat.

How many essential items of equipment to be carried on a sailboat can you recall?

Gudgeons—Female fittings on the transom to which the pindles on the rudder connect.

There are many other items which are used on larger boats and also with spinnaker gear. These can be learned at a later date!

EQUIPMENT

There is numerous equipment or extra gear that can be carried on a sailboat. But, this equipment is broken down into two categories: essentials and non-essentials.

The essentials are:

1. Bilgepump or bailer.
2. Tools—At least screwdriver and pliers.
3. Anchor.
4. Flashlight.
5. Life Jacket—One for each hand aboard.
6. Paddle.
7. Whistle or horn.
8. Bucket or sponge.
9. Extra line.
10. First aid kit.
11. Compass.

Some of the non-essentials include:

1. Outboard engine.
2. Binoculars.
3. Portable radio.
4. Foul-weather gear.
5. Bumpers or fenders.

13

The Language of
Sailing—Glossary

To a person who has never before been around sailboats or sailors, nautical terms and their meanings are very strange and unusual. But, to a sailor, they are very usual and meaningful.

The strange terms we use today were once everyday words in all coastal towns. Since the sails have disappeared from the high seas, many words have disappeared with them. But many have survived through the centuries and a few of these are listed here.

Abeam—At right angles to the fore-and-aft centerline of the boat.

Adrift—A boat which is floating free, not made fast to any object is said to be adrift or drifting.

Aft—Towards the stern.

Backstays—Rope or wire cable leading aft from the mast for the purpose of supporting this spar.

Bail—To remove water from a boat.

Ballast—Heavy material, lead or iron, placed in the bottom of some boats to give stability.

Beam—The maximum width measurement of a vessel.

Bearing—The direction of one object from another.

Beat—To sail to windward.

Bend—To secure or to make fast a sail to a spar. Also the knot by which one rope is made fast to another.

Bilge—Bottom part of the hull adjacent to the keel.

Bow—Front end of a boat.

Broach—A vessel running downwind swings broadside to the wind. Dangerous in high seas.

Centerboard—The flat, board-like object amidships one lowers into the water when sailing.

Chain Plates—Metal plates bolted to the side of the boat to which the stays are attached.

Chock—A metal casting, usually at the bow, through which the mooring line is led.

Cleat—A wood or metal fitting with horns to which lines are secured. Cam or jam cleats provide quick release.

Clew—The lower, aft corner of a sail.

Close Hauled—Sailing as close to the wind as possible.

Cockpit—Open area behind the mast where crew and skipper sit. Some are self-draining.

Come About—To change from one tack to another by turning the bow into the wind.

Cringle—A metal or rope eye sewn into the sail at clew, tack or head, to which sheet or halyard is attached by means of a shackle.

Cuddy—A decked shelter, smaller than the cabin, for protection of the crew aft of the mast.

Daggerboard—A metal or wooden board extending through a boat's bottom; similar to a centerboard.

Downhaul—Block and tackle which pulls down the mainsail to improve its shape when hoisted.

Draft—The depth of water a boat requires to float free of the bottom.

Ease—To let out on the sheet so as to relieve the pressure on the sail and perhaps spill some wind.

Fairlead—An eyelet fitting which changes the direction of a sheet or halyard led through it.

Foot—Lower edge of a sail.

Forward—Towards the bow.

Freeboard—That part of the vessel above the water.

Furl—To roll a sail snugly on boom or yard.

Gaff—A spar used to support the head of the mainsail, hence gaff-rigged, an older type of rigging.

Gear—A general term referring to any item of material or equipment on a boat such as buckets, rope, line, bailing equipment, etc.

Genoa—A large, overlapping jib first introduced in an international 6-meter race at Genoa, Italy.

Gooseneck—A metal fitting, usually a universal joint, securing the boom to the mast.

Gudgeon—An eye fitting into which the rudder's pintles are inserted. Located on the transom of small sailboats.

Gunwale—The rail of the boat at deck level.

Halyard—Rope or wire used to hoist sails.

Hard-A-Lee—Final command sounded as a boat begins to come about. First command is "Ready about."

Hatch—An opening in the deck, with a cover, for access to the cabin below.

Head—The top corner of a sail. Also a toilet.

Headstay—The forward stay supporting the mast. Also called jibstay or forestay. Some boats have both.

Head-To-Wind—Bow headed into the wind, sails luffing.

Head Up—To turn the bow of a boat toward the axis of or into the wind.

Headway—Forward motion of the boat.

Heel—The tilt or tipping action caused by wind.

Helm—The rudder or tiller steering the boat.

Helmsman—The person who is steering a boat.

Hike—To climb or lean out to windward, counteracting excessive heeling of the hull.

Irons—When tacking, a boat that will not come about but lays head-to-wind is said to be in irons.

Jibe—To change tacks by turning away from the wind.

Jibe Ho—Notification that the boom is about to cross the boat when jibing.

Jibstay—Forward stay on which the jib is hoisted.

Jigger—The shorter mast aft on a yawl or ketch.

Keel—The lowest part of the hull, the backbone of the ship, running its entire length.

Leeward—Away from the direction of the wind.

Leech—The after edge of a sail.

Luff—Forward edge of a sail. Also to sail the boat closer to the wind so air will spill from the sails.

Mizzen—The shorter mast aft on a yawl or ketch.

Mooring—The chain or rope, buoy and anchor to which a boat is secured when not sailing.

Off the Wind—Sailing any course except one to windward, which is called "on the wind."

Outhaul—Line and fitting used to secure clew of a sail.

Overstand—To sail beyond an object, such as a buoy.

Painter—Short line used to secure the bow to a landing.

Pinch—To sail a boat too close to the wind.

Pointing—Sailing close to the wind.

Port—The left side of a boat when looking forward from the stern.

Quarter—Side of boat aft of the beam, forward of stern.

Reach—A point of sailing when crossing the wind—between a run and a beat.

Reeve—To pass lines through block or fairlead.

Roach—Outward curve of the leech of a sail.

Running—Sailing before the wind.

Shackle—A U-shaped metal fitting with a pin or screw across the open end, used to join sheets to sails.

Sheet—Line used to trim sails.

Shrouds—Wire or ropes supporting the mast.

Spar—Term for masts, booms, spinnaker poles, etc.

Spreader—Horizontal strut on the mast for its support.

Stand By—1. Make ready. 2. Wait.

Starboard—The right side of a boat when looking forward from the stern.

Stern—Back end of a boat.

Tack—Lower, forward corner of a triangular sail. Also a boat tacks when it changes its direction and the angle at which the wind strikes its sails.

Tender—A sailboat lacking stability, opposite of stiff.

Transom—The stern facing of the hull.

Traveler—Metal rod at stern for trimming mainsail.

Trim—To set the sails at the correct angle to the wind.

Vang—A line to steady the boom when off the wind.

Evaluation Questions

Can you name the terms opposite in meaning to these: windward; aft; running; leech?

Weather—1. To windward. 2. Toward the wind direction.

Whisker-Pole—A light pole or stick extending from the mast and used to hold the jib out when off the wind.

Wind Direction—The direction *from* which the wind is blowing.

Windward—Toward the wind, opposed to leeward.

Index for Canoeing

Index for Sailing